DATE DUE

Lights of Winter

WINTER CELEBRATIONS
AROUND THE WORLD

by Heather Conrad

Illustrated by deForest Walker

Lightport Books
PO·Box 7112
Berkeley, CA 94707

Lightport Books
PO Box 7112
Berkeley, CA 94707

ISBN 0-9712425-1-8

Library of Congress Control Number: 2001092442

For David,
and all the children of the world

✳

With special thanks to Kate Colwell
for the idea for this book,
and to Alisyn Kindle
for all her support.

*L*ong, long ago, before people lived in nice warm houses with heaters and electric lights, the winter was a cold and scary time. The sun only came out a short time each day and people couldn't go outside after the sun set. It was too dark.

People thought the sun disappeared because it was angry with them. So they gathered together and lit many fires and prayed for the sun to come back and warm them again.

And it worked. Every spring the sun came back to warm the Earth. Since that time, all around the world, in winter people have festivals of light to remember that spring is coming.

ZAGMUK

* * * * *

*T*he oldest winter festival is *Zagmuk*. The ancient people of Mesopotamia believed they must make sunlight conquer darkness every winter. In December, they lit many fires and staged a battle between the sun and the monsters of the night.

YULE

* * * * *

The darkest day of the year in the north part of the world is Winter Solstice. Long ago in England, Pagan people gathered in the woods on the night of the Solstice—December 21st. They brought a sacred log—a *Yule* log—to start a great fire. They sang and celebrated to wake up the sun so its warm light would return to them.

SATURNALIA

* * * * *

In ancient Rome there was a festival at the time of Winter Solstice. It was called *Saturnalia*. Friends gave one another candles and there were gifts for every child. Holly berries and pine tree branches decorated homes, reminding everyone of the green plants of spring. Candles and fires glowed as sacred flames to bring back the sun.

SOYAL

* * * * *

The Hopi Indians of America have always celebrated Winter Solstice. They call it *Soyal*. For twenty days, in the *kivas*—underground rooms—Hopi priests pray in the firelight for the sun to return. Then there is a feast and a dance of *kachinas*. They bless the homes with prayer sticks decorated with feathers. A *kachina* in a turquoise helmet walks like a baby to remind people of the birth of the new year and the spring.

TENG CHIEH

* * * * *

*E*very winter for over two thousand years Chinese people have celebrated the beginning of the new year. The holiday lasts fifteen days and the very last day is *Teng Chieh*—Feast of Lanterns. That night people carry colorful lanterns into the streets and walk in a parade. At the front is a giant dragon made of bamboo, paper and silk. The dragon represents strength to bring back the sun.

HANUKKAH

* * * * *

Over two thousand years ago, Jewish people began celebrating *Hanukkah* every December. For eight days they honor the time they fought for their temple and won. After the battle there was only a little oil to light the temple lamps. Then a miracle happened and the oil lasted eight days. Now Jewish people around the world celebrate *Hanukkah* by giving gifts and sharing good food. Children play with wooden tops called *dreidels*. And they light one candle in the *menorah* each of the eight nights.

DIWALI

* * * * *

In the country of India, every year there is a Festival of Lights called *Diwali*. Schools are closed so children can make lanterns called *deepas*. They pour oil into clay bowls and cut string for wicks. They put lanterns on roofs and shelves and pathways. For five days the lanterns light up the dark. The lights honor peace between all sisters and brothers who feast together on the last day of *Diwali*.

CHRISTMAS

* * * * *

Many hundred years ago in Europe, Emperor Constantine changed the Winter Solstice holidays to a celebration of the birth of Jesus Christ. It became *Christmas.* Now on December 25th schools close and people visit family and friends and exchange gifts. Trees are decorated with lights and ornaments. Pine wreaths and holly berries on doorways welcome visitors. On *Christmas,* Christian people give thanks for the arrival of the new baby, Jesus.

LAS POSADAS

* * * * *

In Mexico there is a Christmas tradition called *Las Posadas*. For eight nights people walk from house to house in a parade like the time Joseph and Mary, the parents of Jesus, traveled to Bethlehem. When they arrived, Mary and Joseph asked at people's homes if they could come inside and rest but no one let them in. Finally, on Christmas Eve, someone let them stay in a stable so Jesus could be born. For *Las Posadas* neighbors invite each other in. They light candles, serve food and celebrate.

KWANZA

* * * * *

A very old African harvest celebration has become the winter holiday of *Kwanza* for African-Americans. Family and friends share gifts, good food, music and stories. The candle lighting ceremony begins December 26th. A candleholder called a *kinara* has seven candles, three red, three green and one black for the colors of the African flag. Each day until January 1st a candle is lit to celebrate one of the seven ideas of community and family that the *Kwanza* tradition honors.

Whatever your tradition, when the world gets dark and cold in winter, it can be fun to light candles and lights and to share food and gifts with family and friends. It is fun to celebrate light in the world wherever you see it!